Mama, I Will Send You a Purple Flower

Written and Illustrated by

Manizeh Mirza-Gruber, M.D.

Copyright ©2024 Manizeh Mirza-Gruber, M.D.
Written and Illustrated by Manizeh Mirza-Gruber, M.D.

Photo of Manizeh Mirza-Gruber, M.D. by Nelson Gruber
Photo of Cuddles by her Mama - Manizeh Mirza-Gruber, M.D.

Published by Miriam Laundry Publishing Company
miriamlaundry.com

All rights reserved. This book or any portion thereof may not be reproduced or used in any manner whatsoever without the express written permission from the author except for the use of brief quotations in a book review.

Houston, Texas
Library of Congress Control Number: 2024920463

HC ISBN 978-1-77944-189-8
PB ISBN 978-1-77944-188-1
e-Book ISBN 978-1-77944-187-4

FIRST EDITION

To my parents and sisters for teaching me about forever love.

To my children, Ranya and Aryeh, for being my inspiration to write and illustrate children's books, and for being the best doggy siblings.

To my husband, Nelson, for supporting me in all my endeavors, believing in my wildest dreams, and being an amazing doggy Daddy.

To Lani and Kai, you make my world even more beautiful every day.

To Mila and Aspen, you bring me so much joy.

And to my darling, beloved Cuddles. You are and always will be my shining star, my Cuddles Sitara. Thank you, my baby girl, for allowing me to be your Mama. Thank you for rescuing me.

For all rescue animals. May we continue to provide you with shelter and care. May this book be the first of many written by me to help provide you with a home.

For all you readers, especially children. May you look, believe, and find your own Purple Flower.

It was a cold Thanksgiving Sunday. I hid in the back of the pen at the local animal shelter. I was scared.

I heard a woman's soft voice say to the man at the shelter. "Please, can I look at this litter of seven puppies?"

The man said I had to stay in the shelter for two more days to get my shots and a check-up before I could leave.

Two days later Mama came back for me, and I met my daddy, big sister, and big brother.

Mama said, "Your name is Cuddles Sitara, and you're home now. This is your forever home. You're safe with us. We love you."

I love my new name Cuddles Sitara! I love my Mama! I love my Daddy! I love my sister and brother! I love my forever home!

I loved playing outside in the backyard, chasing my family, and chewing my toys. Sometimes, I chewed ones I wasn't supposed to chew! But Mama was always kind. She always said, "Good girl, Cuddles!"

I loved to run! When I was old enough,
Mama took me on her runs.
It was so much fun keeping up with Mama!

I looked after the house and barked when someone came to the door.

"It's okay, Cuddles," Mama said. "But thank you for protecting us."

One day I ate chocolate cupcakes!
I didn't know chocolate isn't good for doggies!
Mama was so worried when Daddy took me to the doggy doctor.
They said I was okay, and Mama was happy.

Sometimes, Mama was sad, and I licked her salty tears. "I love you so much, my Cuddle Bugs!" Mama said. I loved it when she called me that.

When my big sister and brother went to college, I was sad.
Mama held me and said, "I will always be with you, Cuddle Bugs."

It was fun to go visit my big sister and brother at college.
We stayed in a hotel and ate eggs and pancakes!

When I was almost thirteen years old, Hurricane Harvey came to Houston. Our house was badly damaged, and we had to leave. We stayed together in an apartment for thirteen months! Mama took very good care of me.

Mama knew I did not like to stay alone.
When she went to work, Daddy took me with
him to the house while it was being fixed.

He worked in an office upstairs and I had fun staying next to him.

Then one morning at the apartment, I woke up and didn't feel well. Mama and Daddy took me to see the doggy doctor.

Mama stayed next to me all day, holding me.

Later that afternoon, it was time for me to say goodbye and go to doggy heaven.

Mama and I looked into each other's eyes, just like the first time.

Goodbye, Mama, I told her. *I love you.*

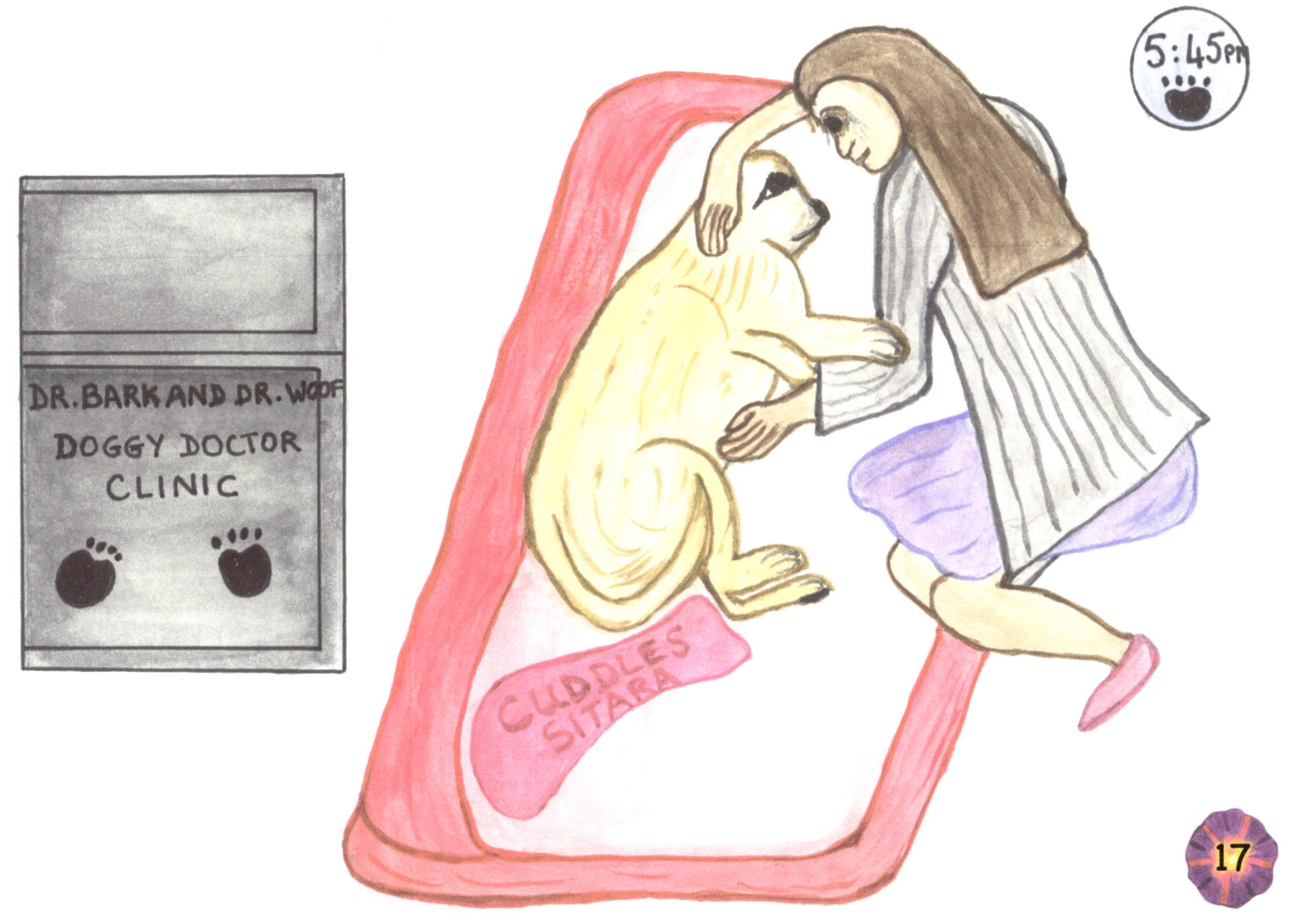

Mama was very, very sad and visited me every day in my special place in the backyard. She whispered, "You're back in your forever home now, Cuddle Bugs. You're safe."

I didn't want to see Mama sad.
I knew I had to do something for her.

*Mama, I will send you a Purple Flower.
It will be okay. I love you.*

Two weeks later, the most beautiful Purple Flower blossomed on the vine next to me.

This was the first time it had ever blossomed!

Mama saw the Purple Flower and loved it! I had made her happy! Every few months I sent her another Purple Flower.

One day, I knew that Mama was ready for another dog. But Daddy had not been well and was now allergic to doggy hair. This time they needed a puppy who did not shed. Mama and Daddy decided to bring home a Goldendoodle.

Mama, I will send you a Purple Flower.
It will be okay. I love you.

Mama knew a lady who had a litter of Goldendoodle puppies. Mama saw this litter and said, "No, I don't see just the right puppy yet." Mama was sad and disappointed.

I let Mama know it would be okay.

*Mama, I will send you a Purple Flower.
Wait, Mama, wait.*

A few weeks later, the lady called Mama again to see another litter of puppies.

The next day, Mama saw a puppy with purple flowers on her collar. "Purple Flowers!" "She's the one!" Mama exclaimed.

Mama knew this was the right puppy!

The puppy was brown, just like me!
Mama and Daddy called her Lani Grace.

Mama loved Lani, and Lani loved Mama. She stayed with Mama and slept in her lap. She loved the food Mama cooked for her. She loved her new toys! She loved coming to my special place in the garden to visit me.

Two months later, Mama saw TWO Purple Flowers on my special vine.

Mama stopped! She stared! Her heart was beating fast, crying happy tears. Mama knew!

She knew what I had done for her.

Remember Mama?
I said I will send you a Purple Flower.

It will be okay. I love you.

I sent Mama Lani Grace. And I sent Lani Grace to her new forever home with my Mama.

13.8 Mindful Lessons I Learned from Cuddles

Dear Ones, who are reading or being read this book:

Hello. How are you today? I want to share with you a few of the lessons I learned from Cuddles, who lived for 13.8 years. They are ways to practice mindfulness if you wish. May they bring a smile to your face and warm your heart. May this moment be one of ease.

With love and gratitude,

Manizeh

1. **Patience:** If we wait, are steadfast and remain patient, good things will come to us in time.

2. **Being nervous is okay:** Even when we feel nervous and scared, know we are not alone. There is always someone else who also feels what we feel and understands.

3. **Paying attention:** When we take time to stop, listen, notice, we discover beauty and goodness around us and within us.

4. **Making mistakes:** We all make mistakes - sometimes big ones, sometimes small ones. We keep learning from them, allowing them to be our teachers.

5. **Dogs do eat our homework!** And yes, even when they do, homework and other projects can be fixed. Remember, it's not the worst moment even though it feels like it is.

6. **Breathe:** Taking a deep in-breath and a longer, deeper, fuller out-breath helps to calm our heart, mind, and body. Taking long sighs is also helpful. I invite you to practice taking a few belly breaths several times a day.

7. **Acceptance:** We can accept ourselves for who we are, even with our bent tails, loud barks, and when we chew the blinds. No one is perfect. Being imperfect is okay.

8. **Endurance:** We learn to trust we will cross our own finish line. We keep practicing, keep trying, and know it is our race - not somebody else's race - we are running.

9. **No need for comparison:** No two dogs or people are alike. We are each special and beautiful in our own unique ways.

10. **Believe:** See the silver lining in every challenge, even when it's difficult. Allow each one to be our guide and keep believing in the journey, not the outcome.

11. **Kindness:** If someone needs a helping hand, be kind, smile, and ask if they need help. We all need help sometimes; we all can give and receive kindness.

12. **Letting Go:** When it is time to say goodbye and we feel sad, make space for letting go. It is alright to cry - really cry - when we feel sadness.

13. **Synchronicity:** Notice the special signs that may come into our life; they usually enter when we least expect them. Often, they are there for a reason. The Purple Flower was mine.

13.8: The Power of LOVE and GRATITUDE: Cuddles taught me every day about forever love and gratitude – I invite us all, dear ones, to keep our hearts open to loving and being grateful...forever and ever.

About the Author/Illustrator

Manizeh Mirza-Gruber, M.D. is a board-certified psychiatrist (ABPN), and a mindfulness teacher and mentor. She cares deeply about guiding others with kindness and compassion to become their truest selves.

Manizeh loves animals, especially dogs, and grew up with her first dog when she was six years old. She became a 'dog mom' when she adopted Cuddles from a local shelter in November 2004.

Manizeh's Goldendoodle, Lani, and her rescue Husky, Kai, light up her life, and stayed by her side through the whole process of writing and illustrating this book.

Her two grand-dogs, Mila and Aspen, love when their 'Mema' comes to visit and play.

Manizeh always loved reading books to her two children, Ranya and Aryeh. They are the inspiration for her becoming an author. She wants to leave a legacy for children everywhere.

Manizeh lives in Houston with her husband Nelson, Lani and Kai. She is "Paying it Forward with Cuddles." A portion of the sales from each book will be donated to animal rescue shelters providing hope and a home to one rescue at a time.

This book honors and celebrates the twentieth anniversary of the moment Manizeh's eyes and heart met with Cuddles for the first time.

You can follow Manizeh:

🌐 www.mindfulinpractice.com

📷 @mindfulinpractice

f @mindfulinpractice

Printed in the USA
CPSIA information can be obtained
at www.ICGtesting.com
LVHW070410241124
797348LV00007B/160